ALLAH´S NAME I BEGIN WITH,

THE MOST MERCIFUL

THE MOST COMPASSIONATE

PUBLICATIONS

HSBT Publications
17-19 Ombersley Road
Balsall Heath
Birmingham
B12 9UR
UNITED KINGDOM

Email: info@bahutrust.org
Website: www.bahutrust.org

Title: The Real Last Sermon of the Holy Prophet
         (Peace and Blessings of Allāh be upon Him)
Author: Dr. Hafiz Ather Hussain Al-Azhari

ISBN: 978-0-9563568-2-6

Design, Print Production & Marketing:

OUTSTANDING
www.outstanding-media.co.uk
office@outstanding-media.co.uk

The *Real* Last Sermon
of the Holy Prophet ﷺ

THIS WORK HAS COME ABOUT DUE TO THE INSPIRATIONAL
WORDS AND WISDOM OF SYED HASIN AL-DIN SHAH SAHIB,
FOUNDER AND PRINCIPAL OF JAMIA RIZWIYYA ZIA AL-ULUM
(RAWALPINDI, PAKISTAN).

Preface ❧

Hazrat Sultan Bahu Trust (HSBT) is very proud to present this paper, aimed at providing clarification on an issue that has been overlooked. One of the most famous sermons delivered by the Holy Prophet ﷺ was on the occasion of the farewell Hajj, on the plains of Arafa. Erroneously, many believe this was his final address to the Muslims. From the rigorously authenticated hadīth and sīra records, we find that the last public address of the Holy Prophet ﷺ was at al-Madīna al-Munawwara, following his visit to the graveyard at Uhud.

We would like to thank the spiritual founder of HSBT, Shaykh Pir Sultan Fiyaz al-Hassan al-Qadiri and Shaykh Pir Sultan Niaz al-Hassan al-Qadiri for their kind support, invaluable encouragement, advice and guidance to this project. We are grateful and offer our kind supplications for the author Dr. Hafiz Ather Hussain al-Azhari. Our gratitude also extends to the Publications & Research Committee (PRC) and the project manager Imam Hafiz Ghulam Rasool for their timely reviews, feedback and coordination in bringing this completed publication to the reader.

We seek your prayers and support in fulfilling our educational aims and we welcome any positive suggestions to improve and enhance the quality of future publications. Jazakallah Khayr.

Hazrat Sultan Bahu Trust, UK.

About the Author ✍

Dr. Hafiz Ather Hussain al-Azhari is currently a lecturer in the Islamic Sciences at Hazrat Sultan Bahu Trust, Birmingham.

Ather Hussain began his Islamic education by completing the memorisation of the Holy Qur'an at the age of thirteen. After completing his GCSEs he moved to Jamia al-Karam, where he studied Arabic Grammar under the guardianship of M.I.H. Pirzada and Mawlana Abdul-Bari Sahib. In 1995, he travelled to Bhera Sharif, Pakistan, and completed the traditional seminary course with First Class Honours. Here he had an opportunity to be taught directly by Zia al-Ummah Pir Muhammad Karam Shah al-Azhari (may Allah shower His mercy upon him).

Between 1996 and 1999, he studied at Al-Azhar University, Cairo, the oldest seat of Islamic learning in the world. He specialised in Hadith studies, and graduated in BA Principles of Theology in 1999.

Upon returning to England, he joined the University of Birmingham, to study BA Political Science. He graduated with First Class Honours in 2003. In 2006, he completed his Mphil in Theology at the University of Birmingham on the *al-Jami* of al-Khatib al-Baghdadi, and he has completed his PhD (Theology) at the same institution.

Twitter: @hafiz_ather

Introduction ๕

All praise is to Allāh, the Lord of the Worlds. May His blessings descend upon His Beloved Messenger, Muhammad ﷺ.

On his farewell Hajj, the Prophet ﷺ ascended the Mountain of Arafa and delivered a beautiful sermon, surrounded by his devout Companions (may Allāh be pleased with them). In an eloquent address, the Holy Prophet ﷺ ordered Muslims to firmly adhere to the Qur'ān and Sunna, and to treat one another fairly and justly. The Holy Prophet ﷺ said:

يايها الناس الا ان ربكم واحد و ان اباكم واحد الا لا فضل لعربي علي أعجمي و لا لعجمي علي عربي و لا لأحمر علي أسود و لا لأسود علي أحمر الا بالتقوي

> O People! Behold! Indeed your Lord is one. Your forefather
> (Ādam) is one. Behold! There is no superiority of an Arab over a
> non-Arab, nor a non-Arab over an Arab. There is no superiority
> of a white man over a black man, nor a black man over a white
> man. [There is no superiority of one over another] except
> through *taqwā*.[1]

For the large majority of Muslims, this was the last perceived sermon of the Holy Prophet ﷺ. Though the Holy Prophet's sermon at Arafa was undoubtedly one of the largest he ever delivered, it was not his

---

1   *Musnad Ahmad*: the remaining chains of the *Ansār*, hadīth no. 22391.

last public speech to the Muslims. This paper aims to highlight the last public sermon delivered by the Prophet, which he conducted in al-Madīna al-Munawwara. Like the one he delivered at Arafa, this sermon too was full of guidance, insight and wisdom. Additionally, the Holy Prophet used this opportunity to express his confidence that he did not expect his followers to commit *shirk* after him. However, he did fear that Muslims after him would fight over the world and its contents. The hadīth also clearly indicates the true rank and status of the Beloved Prophet ﷺ as given to him by Allāh Almighty.

It is hoped that this hadīth will provide guidance for Muslims of this day and age. Readers will undoubtedly be astonished by the Prophet's intellect and wisdom. Owing to the importance of this sermon, a detailed analysis will be offered of it, as outlined by the great Muslim scholars of the past.

THE HADĪTH OUTLINING
THE PROPHET'S FINAL PUBLIC SERMON

حدثنا عبد الله بن يوسف قال حدثنا الليث قال حدثنا يزيد بن أبي حبيب عن أبي الخير
عن عقبة بن عامر :
أن النبي صلي الله عليه و سلم خرج يوما فصلي علي أهل أحد صلاته علي الميت ،
ثم انصرف الي المنبر فقال : اني فرط عليكم و أنا شهيد عليكم ، و اني و الله لانظر
الي حوضي الان ، و اني أعطيت مفاتيح خزائن الارض أو مفاتيح الارض ، و اني ما
أخاف عليكم أن تشركوا بعدي ، و لكني أخاف عليكم أن تنافسوا فيها .

Abd Allāh ibn Yūsuf informed us: he said, Layth informed us: he said, Yazīd ibn Abī Habīb, from Abū al-Khayr, from Uqba ibn Āmir:

'Indeed the Prophetﷺ left one day and performed *salāh* on the martyrs of Uhud, the *salāh* of the deceased. Then he turned to the pulpit and said:

'Indeed I am preceding you; and I am a witness over you. And indeed, by Allāh, I am undoubtedly looking towards the *hawd* [right] now. And indeed I have been given the keys to the treasures of the earth, or the keys of the earth. And verily, I do not fear that you will commit polytheism after me. But I verily fear you will dispute with one another in it (i.e. the world).'

THE SOURCE OF THE HADĪTH

The above hadīth is taken from *Sahīh al-Bukhārī*, which is deemed as the most authentic source after the Holy Qur'ān. Additionally, the chain for this particular hadīth has been declared as 'the most sound of chains'.[2] Imām Muhammad ibn Ismā'īl al-Bukhārī (d. 256 A.H./870 C.E.)[3] mentioned the hadīth five times in his *Sahīh*: (i) Book of Funeral Prayers[4] (ii) Book of Expeditions (*maghāzī*)[5] (iii) ('Twice in the) Book of Making the Heart Tender (*riqāq*)[6] (iv) Book of Merits (*manāqib*).[7]

Other hadīth masters who have recorded the same prophetic report include (i) Imām Muslim ibn Hajjāj (d. 261/874) in *Sahīh Muslim*[8] (ii) Imām al-Nasā'i (d. 303/915) in *Sunan al-Nasā'ī*[9] (iii) Imām Ahmad ibn Hanbal (d. 241/855) in *Musnad Ahmad.*[10]

---

2   See *Irshād al-sārī sharh Sahīh al-Bukhārī*: Allāma Abū Abbās Shihāb al-Dīn Ahmad ibn Muhammad al-Qastalānī (d. 923/1517), II: 440.

3   A.H. indicates 'After Hijra' and C.E. indicates 'Common Era'.

4   Chapter, the prayer upon the martyr, hadīth no. 1258. See *Fath al-bārī*, Hāfiz Ibn Hajar al-Asqalānī (d. 852/1449), III: 241 (hadīth no. 1344).

5   Chapter, *Uhud* loves us and we love *Uhud*, hadīth no. 3776. See *Fath al-bārī*, Hāfiz Ibn Hajar al-Asqalānī (d. 852/1449) VII: 400-1 (hadīth no. 4042).

6   Chapter, what is warned against from the fruits of the world and dispute within it, hadīth no. 5946 & Chapter, the *hawd* (Pool), hadīth no. 6102. See *Fath al-bārī*, Hāfiz Ibn Hajar al-Asqalānī (d. 852/1449), XI: 275 (hadīth no. 6426) & XI: 537 (hadīth no. 6590).

7   See *Fath al-bārī*, Hāfiz Ibn Hajar al-Asqalānī (d. 852/1449), VI: 691-2 (hadīth no. 3596).

8   Book of superiorities, Chapter: the existence of the Prophet's *hawd* and its description; hadīth no. 4248. See *Sharh Sahīh Muslim*, Imām Muhy al-Dīn ibn Sharf al-Nawawī (d. 676/1277), XV: 68.

9   Book of Funeral Prayers, Chapter, the Prayer upon the martyrs, hadīth no. 1928. This narration does not mention the last part 'And verily, I do not fear that you will commit polytheism after me. But I verily fear you will dispute with one another in it.'

10   The chains of the Shāmīs, the reports of Uqba ibn Āmir, hadīth no. 16705.

We know that this sermon took place after the one he delivered in Arafa for the following reasons:

- The Hajj sermon took place in the fields of Arafa, on the outskirts of Makka in the month of Dhūl-Hajj, 10 A.H/March 632 C.E.[11] The Prophet 🌸 returned to al-Madīna al-Munawwara, where he passed away in the month of Rabī al-Awwal three months later. This sermon was definitely delivered in al-Madīna al-Munawwara because it mentions the final resting place of the martyrs of Uhud; the Mountain of Uhud is on the outskirts of al-Madīna al-Munawwara.

- Secondly, the narrator of the hadīth is Uqba ibn Āmir (may Allāh be pleased with him). In the version mentioned by Imām al-Bukhārī in his *Sahīh*, Uqba states that 'this was my last glimpse of the Messenger of Allāh.'[12] This clearly indicates that the sermon was one of the last acts of the Beloved Prophet 🌸 before he left this world.

- Thirdly, the same report mentioned above includes the words 'like a farewell for the alive and the deceased.' In other words, the Prophet 🌸 meant this to be his farewell address to his followers. His prayer for the martyrs of Uhud was his farewell to the deceased, and his brief speech on the pulpit was the farewell to those still alive. Imām al-Nawawī adds that when the Prophet concluded his sermon, Nawwās ibn Sam'ān reports:

---

11   A.H. denotes 'After Hijra'. C.E. denotes 'Common Era'.

12   *Sahih al-Bukhārī*. See *Fath al-bārī*, Hāfiz Ibn Hajar al-Asqalānī (d. 852/1449), VII: 400-1 (hadīth no. 4042).

We said: 'O Messenger of Allāh! As if this is the farewell advice (*maw'iza*). [13]

Based upon this evidence, it is wrong to claim that the Prophet's sermon in Arafa (during the Hajj) was his farewell speech. History testifies that the Prophet ﷺ lived for at least another three months after Arafa. It is preposterous to claim that the Prophet ﷺ did not make a public speech between this period and his worldly demise.

---

13   *Sharh Sahīh Muslim.* Imām Muhy al-Dīn ibn Sharf al-Nawawī (d. 676/1277), XV: 68.

COMMENTARY ON THIS HADĪTH
FROM THE RENOWNED SCHOLARS

What follows is a brief commentary – part by part – on this particular narration from the classical scholars.

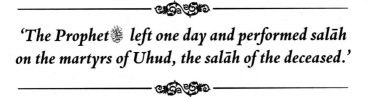

'The Prophet ﷺ left one day and performed salāh on the martyrs of Uhud, the salāh of the deceased.'

Before leaving this world, the Prophet ﷺ said his farewell to the martyrs of the Battle of Uhud. This battle occurred in the month of Shawwāl in the third year of *hijra*.[14]

The *fuqahā* (jurists) dispute whether a martyr is buried and washed like a conventional Muslim deceased. Imām al-Shāfiʻī (d. 204/819), Imām Malik (d. 179/795) and Imām Ahmad (d. 241/855) state that a *shahīd* is not given a bath and the funeral prayer is not performed either. They use the hadīth of Jābir as evidence, in which 'the Prophet ﷺ ordered for their burial (the martyrs of Uhud); they were not washed and the *salāh* was not performed upon them.'[15] Imām Abū Hanīfa states that the funeral prayer is performed upon a *shahīd*. His evidence is the above hadīth, in which the Prophet ﷺ did eventually perform the funeral

---

14   *Umdat al-qārī sharh Sahīh al-Bukhārī*. Allāma Badr al-Dīn al-Aynī (d. 855/1451), VII: 70.

15   *Sahih al-Bukhārī*. Book of funeral prayers; Chapter, the prayer upon the martyr, hadīth 1258. See *Fath al-bārī*, Hāfiz Ibn Hajar al-Asqalānī (d. 852/1449), III: 241 (hadīth no. 1344).

prayer for the martyrs of Uhud.

The narrator of the hadīth Uqba ibn Āmir (may Allāh be pleased with him) clarifies that the *salāh* the Prophet performed was *salāh al-janāza*. This is a refutation of those scholars who believe the word *salāh* in the hadīth means he merely performed a supplication for them, which can also be a form of *salāh*.[16] For instance, Imām al-Nawawī (d. 676/1277) interprets the hadīth to mean that the Prophet ﷺ performed a *duʿā* for them.

The Prophet ﷺ went to Uhud in his final year, but he also used to go there every year to offer his salutations and pray for them:

روي عن ابي شيبة ان النبي صلى الله عليه و سلم كان يأتي قبور الشهداء بأحد علي رأس كل حول

It is reported from Ibn Abī Shayba (d. 235/849) that the Prophet ﷺ would visit the martyrs of Uhud each year.

The four Rightly-Guided Caliphs continued this practice after him. It is upon the basis of such reports that the Ahl al-sunna wa'l jamaʿāt allow the practice of visiting the graves of the pious annually, known as commemorating an *urs*. Clearly therefore, such a practice is not a *bidʿa* but rather the *sunna* of the Messenger and his blessed Companions.

---

16 *Umdat al-qārī sharh Sahīh al-Bukhārī*, VII: 71.

'Then he turned to the pulpit.'

By mentioning the pulpit, the ḥadīth clearly highlights that this sermon of the Prophet ﷺ was a public sermon, rather than a private conversation with some of his Companions. This point is proved further in the narration of Imām al-Bukhārī (found in the Book of Expeditions), where Uqba says 'like a farewell for the living and dead.' His prayer for the martyrs of Uhud was his farewell to the deceased, and his brief speech on the pulpit was the farewell to those still alive.

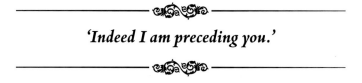

'Indeed I am preceding you.'

The Arabic word used by the Prophet ﷺ here was *farat*. Allāma Badr al-Din Aynī (d. 855/1451) writes that this means 'I am preceding you.' In the olden days, travelling caravans would designate a person to travel faster than the others as the nightfall approached. His task would be to prepare the resting point for when the others reach there. Such a person would be called a *farat*.[17] He would forsake his own comfort and ease for the benefit of others.

In the context of this ḥadīth, it can mean two things:

a. Firstly, it can mean that the Prophet ﷺ was informing his Companions

---

17   *Lisān al-Arab*: Allāma Ibn Manẓūr (d. 711/1311), X: 233.

that he was soon leaving this world. The author of *Irshād al-sarī* writes that 'this was an indication that his passing away was imminent.'[18]

b. Secondly, it can mean that on the Day of Judgement, the Prophet ﷺ will precede his followers and will wait for them at the *hawd* (the Pool of the Prophet).

The latter opinion is more correct, because in one variation of the report, Uqba (may Allāh be pleased with him) narrates that the Prophet ﷺ said: 'I am preceding you at the *hawd*.'

By nature, a *farat* is a selfless person because he thinks about others rather than himself. Our Messenger ﷺ always thought about his followers first and did all he could to ensure our ease and salvation.

'I am a witness over you.'

The Prophet ﷺ used the word *shahīd* here, or 'witness'. Allāma Qastalānī (d. 923/1517) writes:

> [It means] 'I am a witness over your actions.' Thus it is as if he still remains with his followers. He has not proceeded ahead of them but rather remains with them to the extent he witnesses the actions of the last of his followers. Thus the Prophets is overlooking their matter in both worlds, during his life and after his life. It is in the hadīth of Ibn Mas'ūd (may Allāh be

---

18 *Irshād al-sarī sharh Sahih al-Bukhārī*: II: 440.

pleased with him) recorded by [Imām] al-Bazzār, with a fair chain[19] that the Prophet said: 'My living is good for you and my dying is good for you. Your actions are presented to me. Thus whatever I see from good [actions], I praise Allāh for it. And whatever I see from sin, I seek forgiveness from Allāh for you.'[20]

From Ibn Mas'ūd's hadīth, we learn that even after his worldly demise, the Beloved Prophet ﷺ still continues to pray for us and seek forgiveness on our behalf. Furthermore, by using the noun *shahīd* (rather than *shāhid*), the Prophet ﷺ implicitly implied that he was *ever*-watchful over the affairs of his followers, at all times. This is because in Arabic grammar, the word *shahīd* is *sifa mushabbaha*, which gives the meaning of a permanent attribute.

This is the correct interpretation of the Prophet ﷺ as *hāzir* and *nāzir*. He does not have to be everywhere to know what his *ummah* is doing. He does not have to have godly attributes to know what is happening, only God-given ones.

'And indeed, by Allāh, I am undoubtedly looking towards the hawd [right] now.'

Abd Allāh ibn Amr ibn al-Ās (may Allāh be pleased with him) reports that the Prophet ﷺ described the *hawd* as being a square pool; each side is equal to the distance covered in one month's travel. Its water

---

19 In other words, a *sanad* declared as *hasan*.

20 *Irshād al-sārī sharh Sahih al-Bukhārī*, II: 440.

is described as being extremely white, sweeter than honey and more beautifully fragranced than musk perfume. The Prophet ﷺ said that whosoever drinks from the *hawd* will never feel thirst ever again.[21]

Qāḍī Iyād (d. 544 /1149) writes that:

> The *ahādīth* related to the *hawd* are correct and belief in it is compulsory (*fard*). Believing in the *hawd* is a part of one's faith. The *hawd* is to be taken literally; it is not interpreted or disputed.[22]

In this last sermon, the Messenger ﷺ left no room for doubt that he was most certainly looking at the *hawd* as he delivered his words on the pulpit in al-Madīna al-Munawwara. This is proved from a grammatical point of view by the fact he used *innī* twice in the sentence (which means 'verily'), he took an oath with Allāh (*wallāhe*) and the additional *la* on the verb *anzuru* that also gives the meaning of emphasis. As Ibn Ḥajar al-Asqalānī (d. 852/1449) writes, 'the text contains an oath to stress the importance of the information and its revered nature.'[23]

Allāma Badr al-Din Aynī writes that 'it is as if the *hawd* was unveiled for him in that state.'[24] He adds that:

> And in this is a miracle of the Holy Prophet ﷺ in that he saw it in this world and informed others of it.[25]

---

21   *Sahīh al-Bukhārī*: Book of *riqāq*, Chapter: the *hawd*, hadīth no. 6093.

22   Cited in *Sharh Sahih Muslim*: VIII: 53.

23   *Fath al-bārī sharh Sahih al-Bukhārī*: Hāfiz Ibn Hajar al-Asqalānī (d. 852/1449), III: 241.

24   *Umdat al-qārī sharh Sahīh al-Bukhārī*: VII: 71.

25   *Umdat al-qārī sharh Sahih al-Bukhārī*: VII: 71.

Allāma al-Qastalānī adds that this was a 'real vision (*nazar haqīqī*) by the means of unveiling (*kashf*).'[26]

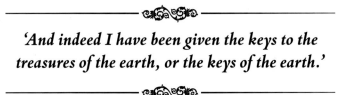

'And indeed I have been given the keys to the treasures of the earth, or the keys of the earth.'

The Companion Uqba (may Allāh be pleased with him) was not sure whether the Prophet ﷺ said 'the keys to the treasures of the earth', or 'the keys to the earth.' Both versions equally highlight the extent of Allāh's favour upon His Beloved Prophet ﷺ.

The fact that the Messenger ﷺ was given the keys to the treasures of the earth explains why water could miraculously gush from his fingers when the Companions were short of water. It explains why the moon split as he pointed to it and how he could travel from Makka to Jerusalem on the Night of Ascension so swiftly.

It is also important to note the passive verb in this sentence ('I have been given…'). All of the Messenger's perfect attributes are given from Allāh Almighty. If the Prophet possesses outstanding knowledge of both worlds, then this is because of Allāh's favour upon him. The Qur'ān states:

> And Allāh taught you what you did not know. And ever great is the grace of Allāh upon you (4: 113).

---

26 *Irshād al-sārī Sharh Sahih al-Bukhārī*: II: 440.

'And verily, I do not fear that you will commit polytheism after me. But I verily fear you will dispute with one another in it (i.e. the world).'

Allāma Badr al-Din Aynī (d. 855/1451) writes that the Holy Prophet ﷺ expressed his confidence that on a general and collective basis, his followers would not commit *shirk* after him. As for individual cases, the Prophet ﷺ did not give such a guarantee.[27]

The word used in the hadīth is *tanāfasū*, which means desire and selfishness. The Prophet ﷺ said he feared Muslims would have an inclination to the world and would desire its contents for themselves, to the exclusion of others. As for *shirk*, the Prophet ﷺ remarked that he was not concerned that his followers would resort to it after his demise.

Needless to say, this is a clear refutation of some Muslims today who decree the acts of devout Muslims as *shirk* without proof and evidence. If the Prophet ﷺ did not fear his followers would fall into the sin of polytheism in general, what authority do these Muslims have to declare others as *mushrik*s?

Perhaps more importantly, it is a grave insult to the Messenger ﷺ if it is assumed that *shirk* is still widespread. The reason is because this then implies that the appearance of the Messenger had little or no effect on humanity, that *shirk* was prevalent before his appearance and *shirk* still

27 *Umdat al-qārī sharh Sahih al-Bukhārī*, VII: 71.

continued after he left this world. This perspective is wholly incorrect. Rather, Muslims rightly believe that no individual had more impact on humanity than the Mercy of the worlds, peace and blessings of Allāh be upon him.

Conclusion ﷽

The aim of this paper was *not* to lessen the importance of the Arafa sermon. This sermon was a thousand years ahead of its time. As recent as the 1960s, the Deep South of the USA would have different water fountains for whites and blacks. Racial segregation was considered perfectly normal. The Prophet's sermon was ground-breaking in the manner it aimed to eradicate any sense of prejudice based on colour, gender, ethnicity and race.

Rather, the aim of this paper was to highlight what is factually and empirically correct; this was the last public address of the Holy Prophet ﷺ, the one delivered in al-Madīna al-Munawarra. It is a tragedy that very few of us are aware of this sermon. An argument could be made to suggest that some Muslims have *deliberately* covered up the importance of the sermon delivered in al-Madīna al-Munawwara. After all, the Prophet ﷺ stated here that he did not fear *shirk* would be prevalent in his *ummah*, that he is ever-watchful over us, and that he has been given immense superiority from his Lord.

To conclude, what did the Holy Prophet ﷺ say?

Realise how much I care for you. This is why he described himself as a *farat*; someone concerned about the welfare of others.

Realise how concerned I am for you. This is why he described himself as a *shahīd*, someone who would be ever-aware and mindful of our actions.

Realise my God-given status. The *hawd* and the keys to the treasures of the earth are only two ways that our Messenger has been blessed immensely by Allāh Almighty.

Realise my contribution to mankind. This is how his guidance led to the eradication of *shirk*.

ৰ

Dr. Hafiz Ather Hussain al-Azhari.

BA Principles of Theology, al-Azhar University, Cairo, Egypt.

MA Arabic and Islamic Studies, Dar al-Ulum Muhammadia Ghawsia, Bhera, Pakistan.

BA Political Science, MPhil Theology & PhD Theology, University of Birmingham.

Bibliography ૐ

Fath al-bārī sharh Sahih al-Bukhārī: Shaykh al-Islām Hāfiz Ibn Hajar al-Asqalānī (d. 852/1449). Dār al-Hadīth Publications, Cairo, 2004.

Irshād al-sārī sharh Sahīh al-Bukhārī: Allāma Abū Abbās Shihāb al-Dın Ahmad ibn Muhammad al-Qastalānī (d. 923/1517). Dār al-Kitāb al-Arabiyya Publications, Beirut, 1984.

Lisān al-Arab: Allāma Ibn Manzūr (d. 711/1311). Dār Ihyā al-Turāth al-Arabī Publications, Beirut, 1988.

Sharh Sahīh Muslim: Imām Muhy al-Dīn ibn Sharf al-Nawawī (d. 676/1277). Mu'assassat al-Mukhtār, Cairo, 2001.

Umdat al-qārī sharh Sahīh al-Bukhārī: Allāma Badr al-Dīn al-Aynī (d. 855/1451). Mustafā al-Bābī al-Halbī Publications, Egypt, 1972.

HSBT SPONSORSHIP FOR PUBLICATIONS

❧

Hazrat Sultan Bahu Trust (HSBT) offers the following sponsorship schemes for its publications:

> **Isaale Thawab sponsorship scheme for the deceased**
> On the occasions of funerals and death anniversaries (*khatam*), promoting the message that books are an effective and long term substitute for langhar. This service can be done discreetly too.

> **Named sponsors scheme**
> Stickers for sponsoring organisations, promotion of individuals or organisations with a provision to additionally publicise these on HSBT websites & social media outlets.

Sponsorship scheme details:

- 100% full cost sponsorship of a complete print run.

- Limited quantity specific publications scheme i.e. 100, 200, 300 or 786, 1100, 1200 units.

- Limited percentage based print run scheme i.e. 25% or 50% or 75% sponsorship of a publication run.

Sponsorship incentives and benefits:

- Specific & dedicated page mentioning sponsor(s) or, sponsoring organisation(s), the person(s) who the Isaale Thawab is intended for.

- As well as highlighting your organisation(s) and person(s), including a message and du'a.

- Publicise sponsor(s) and Isaale Thawab person(s) on Takbeer TV, websites & social media outlets to remind of a loved one(s) to the Muslim Ummah and sharing our strong connection and support for them even after death.

Such high-quality publications will require financial support, and we would like to attract sponsors to get involved in this worthy cause. For donors and sponsors this will be a great method of tabligh & da'wah in this world and a strong form of investment in thawab for the Hereafter, both for themselves and their loved ones.

HSBT Publications and Research Committee (PRC)
Tel: **0121 440 4096**

܀

Hazrat Sultan Bahu Trust UK (HSBT) is an international educational and spiritual missionary movement that is committed to serving humanity through the guidance & teachings of Allah and His Final Messenger Prophet Muhammad ﷺ. It is at the forefront in promoting tasawwuf (sufism), the spiritual dimension of Islam, with a special focus on the teachings of the renown saint Hazrat Sultan Bahu ﵌.

Under the leadership of Shaykh Pir Sultan Fiaz al-Hassan Qadiri and Shaykh Pir Sultan Niaz ul-Hassan Qadiri, HSBT has established dozens of centres in the UK since 1983 and runs hundreds of educational projects throughout the world.